FORMS OF GOVERNMENT: NEED TO KNOW

THEOCRACY

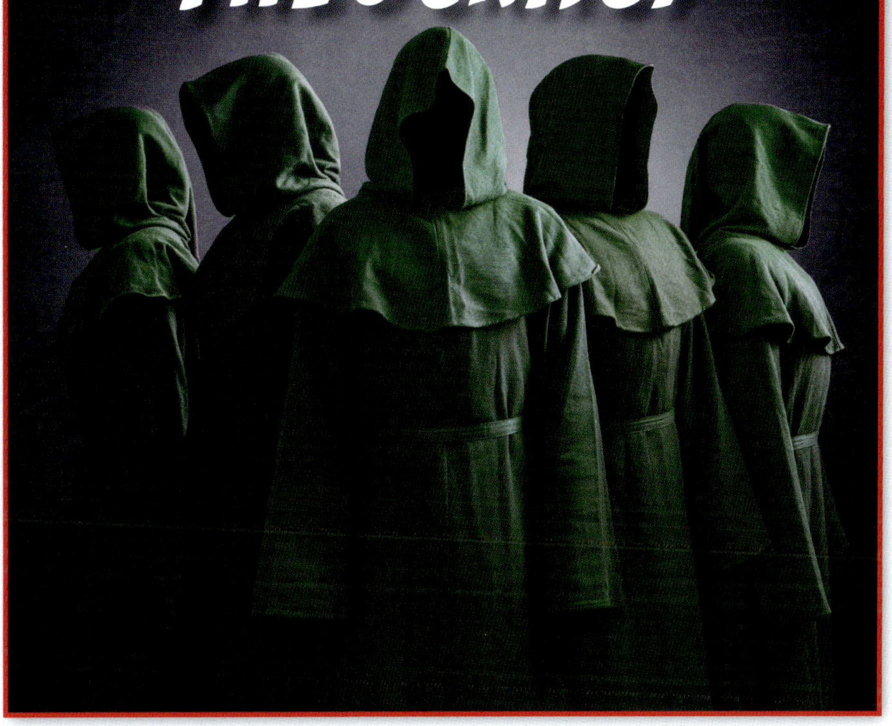

by D. R. Faust

Consultant: Caitlin Krieck, Social Studies Teacher and Instructional Coach, The Lab School of Washington

SilverTip Books, an imprint of Bearport Publishing by FlutterBee

Credits
Cover and title page, © Jakub Krechowicz/Adobe Stock; 3, © PeskyMonkey/Shutterstock; 5T, © AJR_photo/Shutterstock; 5M, © stockpexel/Shutterstock; 5B, © Odua Images/Shutterstock; 7, © Brandon Laufenberg/iStock and © vectorlight/Shutterstock; 9, © Jakub Krechowicz/Shutterstock; 11T, © Rawpixel.com/Shutterstock; 11B, © shulers/Shutterstock; 13, © Peter Probst/Alamy Stock Photo; 14–15, © DCProduction Media/Shutterstock; 17, © robertharding/Alamy Stock Photo; 19, © robertharding/Alamy Stock Photo; 21, © incamerastock/Alamy Stock Photo; 22–23, © Alexander Sviridov/Shutterstock; 25, © Salvacampillo/Shutterstock; 27, © Rocco Pettini/Shutterstock; 28L, © ZUMA Press, Inc./Alamy Stock Photo; 28M, © WENN Rights Ltd/Alamy Stock Photo; 28R, © Marco Iacobucci Epp/Shutterstock.

Bearport Publishing Company Product Development Team
Kayla Eggert, Theresa Emminizer, Kim Jones, Allison Juda, Cole Nelson, Naomi Reich, Steve Scheluchin, Tiana Tran

Statement on Usage of Generative Artificial Intelligence
Bearport Publishing remains committed to publishing high-quality nonfiction books. Therefore, we restrict the use of generative AI to ensure accuracy of all text and visual components pertaining to a book's subject. See BearportPublishing.com for details.

Library of Congress Cataloging-in-Publication Data is available at www.loc.gov or upon request from the publisher.

ISBN: 979-8-89577-639-1 (hardcover)
ISBN: 979-8-89577-793-0 (paperback)
ISBN: 979-8-89577-727-5 (ebook)

For more information, write to Bearport Publishing, 3500 American Blvd W, Suite 150, Bloomington, MN 55431. Printed in the United States of America.

Contents

Church and Government

Many people belong to a religion. It may help them form their beliefs. Often, it can give people community. But for some, religion goes further. It is part of their government, shaping the laws of the land. This type of government is called a theocracy.

Many countries keep religion and government separate. Their laws are not based on religious beliefs. And people can follow whatever religion they want.

Rule of God

The word *theocracy* comes from ancient Greek. It means rule of god. The Greeks came across this kind of government in ancient Israel and Judah. These were countries in what we now call the Middle East. Here, the rulers said they spoke for god.

For a long time, the Greeks knew of only three types of government. Theocracy became a fourth!

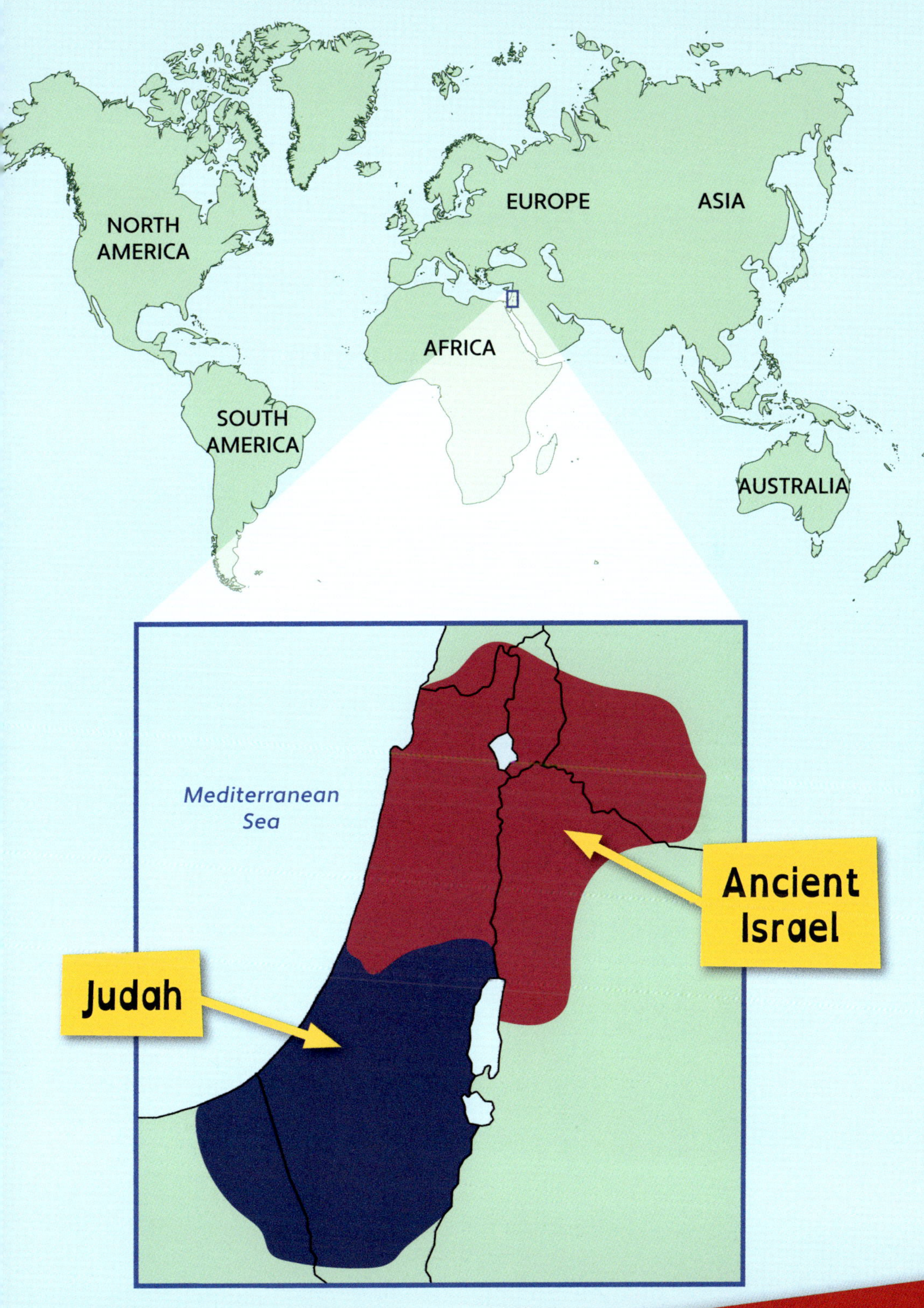
NORTH AMERICA
SOUTH AMERICA
EUROPE
ASIA
AFRICA
AUSTRALIA
Mediterranean Sea
Ancient Israel
Judah

In a theocracy, the **civil** rulers are also religious leaders. There may be a single person or a group in charge. But these leaders say they rule in the name of a god or gods. Religious values shape their laws.

Some countries have state religions. There is an official religion of the country. However, these places may not have a theocracy. Religion may still be separate from shaping other laws.

Holding Power

There are a few kinds of theocracies. The main difference between them is who holds power.

In one type, there are both religious and non-religious leaders. Laws are made by both groups. Non-religious leaders may make laws about taxes. But there could be laws about marriage based on religion.

Constitutional theocracies are formed by a set of laws. These include rules about how religion will be part of the government. However, there may also be non-religious parts of the government.

Tax Form
Document No.38520-1
Personal Details
Last name
Phone Number
No.
Your first name and initial
Nationality
Address (street and number), see instructions.
City, town, street and ZIP code, see instructions.
You
Checking a box for confirmation (See instructions on page 12)
Single
Married
Status
Check only one box.
Income
Dependents:
Last name
Dependent's social security number.

In another kind of theocracy, all power is held by religious leaders. Iran has this kind of government. It is led by the supreme leader. This is the most powerful person in government. They are also at the head of religion.

Iran has a president. But this role has very little power. The supreme leader picks people for government jobs. They control the military. And they can even rewrite laws.

Ali Khamenei is the supreme leader of Iran. He has been since 1989.

It's Divine

Some rulers say their power comes directly from a god or gods. This is called the **divine** right.

The idea of divine right helps these leaders stay in power. Few people question the rulers. For them, it would be like going against a god.

Some of these rulers are even thought to become gods upon death. This was true in the Roman Empire. Some leaders and their families were worshipped after they died.

From Large to Small

There are some national governments that are theocracies. But religious rule is much more common at the local level. People in these kinds of communities often seek out their groups. They join because of shared values.

Small communities that form from shared values are called **communes**. There are both religious and non-religious communes.

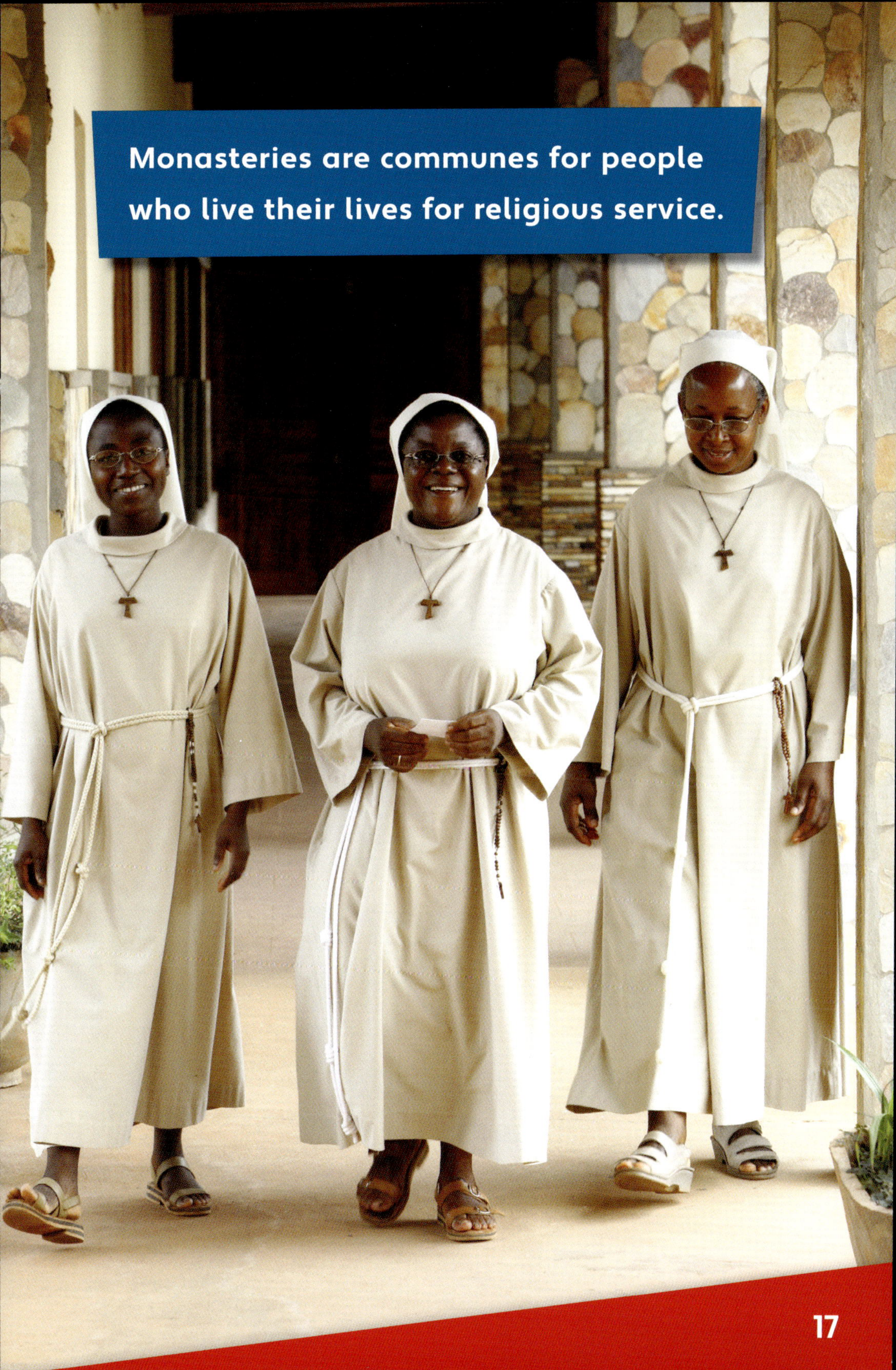

Monasteries are communes for people who live their lives for religious service.

A Long History

Theocracy was common in many ancient **civilizations**. Mesopotamian **city-states** were probably ruled by priest-kings. Likewise, ancient Egypt had this kind of government. Pharaohs were believed to be godlike. They were thought of as a direct connection between people and the gods.

While alive, pharaohs were connected to the god Horus. This changed when pharaohs died. Then, they were said to take the form of the god Osiris.

Ancient Egyptian art often showed pharaohs with gods.

Rulers continued to claim their power came from gods for thousands of years. Emperors of ancient China said their power was a **mandate** of heaven. This meant a god or divine force selected the emperors to rule. Many European kings claimed they had a divine right to rule, too.

The Holy Roman Empire ruled central and western Europe. It was in power for more than 1,000 years. Control of this government was shared. There was an emperor and a pope.

Henry VIII claimed the divine right of kings to hold power over England.

American Theocracies

There is a long history of theocracies in the Americas. The Maya and Aztecs ruled this way. They were around long before the first Europeans came.

When **settlers** arrived, they brought different religious ideas. Some formed communities with shared values. However, many did not set up theocracies for their governments.

Plymouth, Massachusetts

When they lived in Europe, the Pilgrims were harassed for their beliefs. In North America, they formed religious communities. Plymouth, Massachusetts, is the most well known. It was founded in 1620.

Theocracies Today

In modern times, there are several countries ruled with the laws of Islam. These include Afghanistan, Iran, and Saudi Arabia.

Many Tibetans consider their leader to be the Dalai Lama. He is both a religious and political leader.

Dalai Lama is a religious title. It is held by the leader of Buddhism in Tibet. The title is passed down. The current Dalai Lama is the fourteenth.

The Dalai Lama

Vatican City is the smallest city-state in the world. It is also a theocracy. The head of Vatican City is the pope.

Theocracies have stood the test of time. They have been around from the ancient world to today. And they will likely continue going forward.

The pope is the head of the Catholic Church. He runs Vatican City with the help of other religious leaders. They are called the Roman Curia, or the Court of Rome.

Pope
Leo XIV

Forms of Theocracies

All theocracies are governments based on religion. However, there are key differences in how they run.

RELIGIONS

These governments may be based on different religions.

Ali Khamenei leads Islamic Iranians.

Dalai Lama leads Tibetan Buddhists.

Pope Leo XIV leads Catholics in Vatican City.

POWER

The leaders may have different amounts of power or control.

- A single leader with the powerful backing of religion
- Multiple leaders
  - All leaders are religious
  - Power is split between religious and non-religious leaders

SilverTips for SUCCESS

★SilverTips for REVIEW

Review what you've learned. Use the text to help you.

Define key terms

civil
communes
constitutional theocracy
divine right
mandate of heaven

Check for understanding

Name one way that all theocracies are similar.

Describe one way theocracies can be different.

What is one place that had a theocracy in the past and one that has a modern theocracy?

Think deeper

How might your life be affected if you lived under a different form of government?

★SilverTips for TAKING TESTS

- **Make a study plan.** Ask your teacher what the test is going to cover. Then, set aside time to study a little bit every day.
- **Read all the questions carefully.** Be sure you know what is being asked.
- **Skip any questions** you don't know how to answer right away. Mark them and come back later if you have time.

Glossary

city-states states that have their own governments and are made of a city and the surrounding area

civil related to the basic laws of a place

civilizations large groups of people that share the same history and way of life

communes groups that live together based on shared values and responsibilities

divine related to or coming from a god or gods

mandate an official order or command

settlers people who live and make a home in a new place

Read More

Anderson, Shannon. *Iran (Countries of the World).* Minneapolis: Bellwether Media, 2025.

Faust, D. R. *The Rise and Fall of Ancient Egypt (Ancient Civilizations: Need to Know).* Minneapolis: Bearport Publishing, 2025.

Sonneborn, Liz. *Pope Leo XIV: First American Pope (Gateway Biographies).* Minneapolis: Lerner Publications, 2026.

Learn More Online

1. Go to **FactSurfer.com** or scan the QR code below.
2. Enter "**Theocracy**" into the search box.
3. Click on the cover of this book to see a list of websites.

Index

About the Author

D. R. Faust is a freelance writer of fiction and nonfiction. They live in Queens, NY.